RICH RONALD

THE GREATEST GIFTS

A 25-DAY CHRISTMAS DEVOTIONAL

The Greatest Gifts

Copyright©2014 Rich Ronald

ISBN-13: 978-1501001413
ISBN-10: 1501001418

This book is manufactured in the United States.

THE GREATEST GIFTS
by Rich Ronald

MIKE,

THANKS FOR BEING A JOYFUL GIFT TO ME, AND MANY OTHERS!

WITH JOY,

Rich

DEDICATED TO THOSE WHO DESIRE A DEEPER INTIMACY WITH JESUS DURING THIS SEASON WHEN WE CELEBRATE HIS BIRTH.

CONTENTS

The 25 Days of God's greatest gifts, from the book of Ephesians (chapter and verse in parenthesis):

ACKNOWLEDGMENTS

Who doesn't love Christmas? Growing up, we always had an Advent wreath where we lighted candles and read Scripture as a means to prepare our hearts for the coming of the celebration of the birth of Jesus. I'm eternally thankful to my parents, Bill and Jeanne Ronald, for instilling in me a desire to continue this great tradition of faith. And I'm so thankful to my bride, Linda, for her whole-hearted love for Jesus and the ways she has encouraged our family to celebrate His coming.

I'm thankful to my partners in the Gospel at Oak Hills Church in San Antonio, and especially the eldership and lay leaders at the North Central Campus who continue to encourage me to write.

I'm grateful to the best man at our wedding and brother-in-law, Greg Eckel, whose beautiful creativity graces the cover and title pages.

And I'm thankful to those who have come alongside to inspire, edit and offer input, including Lynn Dean.

THE GREATEST GIFTS
GETTING READY

Welcome to Advent, the season that heralds our Lord Jesus and leads up to the celebration of His birth. This devotional will take, perhaps, a slightly different slant to the season as we open Paul's letter to the church at Ephesus. Why Ephesians? Well, you are right to suggest that the book isn't very "Christmasy." There are no stories about trips on donkeys, a baby born in a stable or angels singing outside the window.

However, the book of Ephesians mirrors many writings throughout the Bible. It includes these two main points:

- God loves you and has a plan for you,

- … and that plan has includes the hope and glory and power and wisdom and love of Jesus our Messiah.

Even if you have never bowed your knee to Jesus as your personal Savior and Lord, know that God loves you and has a plan for you. And He has good gifts for you, His child.

So, let's take the month of December, between now and Christmas Day and give Ephesians a closer look. At its core, we'll discover 25 wonderful gifts God desires to give each one of us. They are The Greatest Gifts.

Are you ready to receive them?

A prayer for you from the author and rabbi Paul:

For this reason, ever since I heard about your faith in the Lord Jesus and your love for all God's people, I have not stopped giving thanks for you, remembering you in my prayers. I keep asking that the God of our Lord Jesus Christ, the glorious Father, may give you the Spirit of wisdom and revelation, so that you may know him better. I pray that the eyes of your heart may be enlightened in order that you may know the hope to which he has called you, the riches of his glorious inheritance in his holy people, and his incomparably great power for us who believe. That power is the same as the mighty strength he exerted when he raised Christ from the dead and seated him at his right hand in the heavenly realms, far above all rule and authority, power and dominion, and every name that is invoked, not only in the present age but also in the one to come. And God placed all things under his feet and appointed him to be head over everything for the church, which is his body, the fullness of him who fills everything in every way. (Ephesians 1:15-23 NIV)

The very words of God.

Paul starts this prayer by offering thanksgiving for the people of the church congregation in Ephesus. He asks God to give them all wisdom and revelation so that the people may know God better. And then Paul prays for their hearts. That each may know His hope, His inheritance and His power! And finally he affirms that

that power is the same that raised a dead man to life -- Jesus -- and in its fullness, is available to us ... filling everyone in every way.

You might want to set aside 10-15 minutes each day to read, to ponder, to pray and to receive the gifts that God has for you as you prepare your heart for Christmas this year. We'll begin together in Chapter 1 of Ephesians and work our way through the end of Chapter 6 over the next 25 days. While the scriptures will be listed and there is space for you to write a prayer included at the end of each day, feel free to use your own Bible and journal and let God encourage you and speak to you.

ADVENT DAY

1

YOUR BEST GIFT?

December, Christmas and gifts. They go hand in hand don't they? Do you remember the best gift you've ever received? How about the worst gift?

Sometimes it's a matter of perspective. My sister tells the story of a gift she and her husband gave to each other once. Gutters. Yep, gutters. You might not think that's a very romantic gift. But for this newly married couple building their first home, rain gutters were an extravagant luxury. So it was a delightful welcomed gift for each!

There are things we want and things we need. I believe there are three basic categories of "needs" that we all have:

Physical needs: food, water, a roof over our head, clothes on our backs, tangible things.

Emotional needs: happiness, peace, tranquility. Those are generally easy to identify.

But this third one is sometimes harder to grasp: spiritual needs. What are spiritual needs that we have?

One definition is from a man named Howard Clinebell. He is a clinical psychologist and a university PhD. He says we all have at least seven spiritual needs in our core. The first is this: "All people need to experience regularly the healing and empowerment of love -- from others, from self, and from God."[1]

Love!

Paul says right at the beginning that Jesus **"has blessed us with every spiritual blessing in the heavenly places."** (Ephesians 1:3 NASB) Jesus is the source of spiritual blessings! So it makes sense to me that even the worldly scientist, Dr. Clinebell says that spiritual blessing is love, because we know that 1 John 4:8 says that **"God is love."**

Jesus is the One who gives us the greatest gift we can have … every spiritual blessing. Love!

You know, I can live without physical needs like a house or food, for a while anyway. I can survive without emotional needs. I don't *have* to be happy. I can *choose* to be grumpy. But I would say that none of us can fully live the lives that God has for us without embracing the unlimited spiritual need of love -- provided by the grace-filled hands of Jesus.

And that gets us back to the Greatest Gifts. **"God so loved the world that He gave His one and only son, Jesus, that whoever believes in Him may not be lost but have eternal life."** (John 3:16 NCV)

Open your hands and receive the first gift of the Season -- the Gift of Love, the Gift of Every Spiritual Blessing!

God, thank you for the Gift of Every Spiritual Blessing. Help me receive it with joy. Help me receive Your Love this Season. And help me give joy and love to others. In Jesus' Name, Amen.

Use this space to write a prayer or your thoughts about this Gift:

_____

_____

_____

_____

_____

_____

_____

_____

_____

_____

_____

_____

_____

_____

_____

_____

ADVENT DAY

2

THE GIFT OF BEING ADOPTED AS HIS CHILDREN

Do a Google search on the word "adopted" and you'll find heartfelt story after story of a child being adopted and given a new life when the birth parent(s) would only be able to provide much less. There are countless examples of the famous and obscure enjoying a fresh life thanks to being adopted, to being chosen.

God is the ultimate adoptive parent. He has given us the choice of whether or not we want to be adopted by Him, through His Son. And, being the omnipotent God that He is, He knows what our choice will be while urging each of us to become His child.

The next gift? Adoption. **"In love, he predestined us for adoption to sonship through Jesus Christ."** (Ephesians 1:5 NIV)

Now, some people get hung up on the word "predestined." Some would suggest that if God has predestined whether or not I go to heaven, then I don't need to get caught up in His decision. I can act like I want. And since it is mentioned in several other places in the Bible that God wants everyone to be saved, then I've been predestined to go to heaven. It doesn't matter how I act, right? No, that's not right, is it?

Predestination means God has the plan -- and it's a good and great plan -- but *we* do the choosing whether or not we're going to follow that plan. When we choose

God, we receive the inheritance, like sons and daughters. God's plan for us is clear: **"'For I know the plans I have for you," declares the LORD, "plans to prosper you and not to harm you, plans to give you hope and a future.'"** (Jeremiah 29:11 NIV) So, why wouldn't we want to accept the plan God has for us? It's a great plan. It's a wonderful gift!

John Calvin, one of the great leaders of the Christian faith in the 1500's wrote and preached much on predestination. He suggested that no one can live a Godly life without the Holy Spirit being in him, without God having called that person to be a believer.

Why would a person want to be God's son or daughter? Romans 8 says that God's love for each person is so immense that nothing can contain God's love for us. Calvin wrote: "When we have our adoption engraved in our hearts, then ... we have a good and infallible pledge that God will guide us unto the end, and that since he has begun to lead us into the way of salvation, he will bring us to the perfection to which he calls us, because, in truth, without him we could not continue so much as a single day."[2]

God has called us. God has elected us. **"But as many as received Him, to them He gave the right to become children of God, *even* to those who believe in His name, who were born not of ... the will of man, but of God."** (John 1:12-13 NASB)

God has predestined us to follow Him, to embrace the great things He has for us, to love Him. And I am thankful for that gift. Because with it, He is the One who guides us through this life on our path to spending all of eternity with Him. He guides. We choose.

So gift #2 is the Gift of Adoption, of being called God's son or God's daughter, and all the love that goes with it!

Thank you God, for this Gift of Adoption, of being Your child. I joyfully choose to be your child and receive all the love you give to me as my unfailing Heavenly Father. In Jesus' Name, Amen.

Use this space to write a prayer or your thoughts about this Gift:

_____

_____

_____

_____

_____

_____

_____

_____

_____

_____

_____

ADVENT DAY

3

SEALED WITH THE HOLY SPIRIT

Bank tellers and others who handle money are trained to tell the difference between real currency and counterfeit. The real stuff has markings imbedded in between the fibers of the bills that can be seen when one knows how to examine the currency. Real. Genuine. Authentic.

The third gift is this: **"And you also were included in Christ when you heard the message of truth, the gospel of your salvation. When you believed, you were marked in him with a seal, the promised Holy Spirit, who is a deposit guaranteeing our inheritance until the redemption of those who are God's possession -- to the praise of his glory."** (Ephesians 1:13-14 NIV)

What a gift! To be sealed in Him by the Holy Spirit.

What does it mean to be sealed in God by the Holy Spirit? Think of a letter or edict in the days of Paul. It was common that a king would write a letter on animal skin parchment, roll it up, and then dip his royal signet ring into hot wax and press the wax onto the parchment, sealing the letter, assuring that if anyone opened the letter they would crack the seal. It made the letter authentic. It was certified as coming from the king.

So what happens when God seals you with the Holy Spirit? It makes you authentic. It certifies that you are from God. And that you are protected by God. Whoa! And your life as God has chosen you is to be read by others as someone who is "of God." That is a pretty big responsibility, isn't it? However here's the good news. If you are sealed by the Holy Spirit, and are walking in the ways God calls us to walk, you reflect God naturally. Or perhaps we might say "supernaturally."

Recall that Jesus promised the Holy Spirit to his followers.

> **"But when He, the Spirit of Truth comes, He will guide you into all the Truth. For He will not speak His own message; but He will tell whatever He hears and He will announce and declare to you the things that are to come. He will honor and glorify Me, because He will take of what is Mine and will reveal it to you."** (John 16:13 AMP)

So, the Holy Spirit is leading you into truth. You are reflecting that truth to others. You are sealed. And that seal, **"is given as a pledge of our inheritance."** (Ephesians 1:14 NASB) It's a promise from the King! We are His children. We will spend all eternity with the King. More appropriately, we *are spending* all eternity with the King. He promised it. He sealed it. It's done. What a gift!

Open your hands and receive this gift today -- the Gift of Being Sealed with the Holy Spirit.

Thank you God, for the Gift of Being Sealed with your Holy Spirit. I am your authentic child who represents the King of kings. Protect me and help me reflect You today in all I am and all I do. In Jesus' Name, Amen.

Use this space to write a prayer or your thoughts about this Gift:

_____

_____

_____

_____

_____

_____

_____

_____

_____

_____

_____

_____

_____

_____

_____

ADVENT DAY

4

THE FREE GIFT OF SALVATION

Have you ever received something totally free, with no strings attached? Marketing executives often create advertising campaigns around free giveaways. They're called B1G1F. That's advertising speak for "Buy One, Get One Free!" Or "BOGOFree!" But you know deep down that whatever they are giving away isn't really free, is it? Somebody had to pay for the free product that is being given away, right? That person is usually you, in the form of buying something else in the store at a greater mark up to cover the cost of the free giveaway.

Well, the gift of salvation *is* free for you and me. All we have to do is ask for it and God is quick to give it to us.

Immense in mercy and with an incredible love, he embraced us. He took our sin-dead lives and made us alive in Christ. He did all this on his own, with no help from us! Then he picked us up and set us down in highest heaven in company with Jesus, our Messiah. Now God has us where he wants us, with all the time in this world and the next to shower grace and kindness upon us in Christ Jesus. Saving is all his idea, and all his work. All we do is trust him enough to let him do it. It's God's gift from start to finish! We don't play the major role. If we did, we'd probably go around bragging that

we'd done the whole thing! No, we neither make nor save ourselves. **God does both the making and saving.** (Ephesians 2:4-9, THE MESSAGE)

When you read this, you can't help but see that the gift of salvation is a beautiful gift of faith. Given not because of anything we've done, but because of God's love. He wants to shower grace and kindness upon us. Do you remember a time when someone just showered grace and kindness upon you? Even when you didn't deserve it? Perhaps it was a parent, or a teacher, or a spouse or a close friend.

God gives. We receive.

If you are a giver, sometimes it can be really hard to receive, can't it?

There was a season in my life when I gave and gave and gave. I had this spreadsheet all worked out where I was on track to give away half of my income by the time I turned 50 years old. And then I lost my job. It was my turn to receive. Boy, was that ever a challenge! But God taught me something. In order to truly appreciate the gift, I had to joyfully receive. During this time, an almost complete stranger gave us a couple of thousand dollars. It was a sacrifice for them to give. I didn't want to receive it. But then, I realized that if I minimized the gift, I minimized the giver.

Thanks to Jesus' death on the Cross of Calvary, thanks to His gift of laying down His life, we have the gift of life and life eternal. And if He hadn't been born during this Advent season, He could not have given us this incredible gift.

So open your hands and get down on your knees and receive this most wonderful gift -- the Free Gift of Salvation.

Thank you, God, for the ultimate gift, the Free Gift of Salvation. Please give me a heart that truly appreciates this gift, and the Giver. In Jesus' Name. Amen.

Use this space to write a prayer or your thoughts about this Gift:

_____

_____

_____

_____

_____

_____

_____

_____

_____

_____

_____

_____

ADVENT DAY

5

THE GIFT OF WORK TO DO AT GOD'S REQUEST

Could it be that work is a gift? Absolutely! And not just any work, but work to do for God. Important work. Necessary work.

"For we are His workmanship, created in Christ Jesus for good works, which God prepared beforehand so that we would walk in them." (Ephesians 2:10 NASB)

Now, at first blush this may seem quite contrary to the previous verse of being saved by faith alone. But really it is not. It is actually an affirmation.

Do you know that God has something for you to do today? He has ordained it. Good works, not for our benefit nor even so that we will earn our salvation, but a project, a deed, a word to speak, a hug to give, a stack of dishes to wash, a bed to make or a prayer to offer. Yes, God can rearrange circumstances so that these works, these tasks that we do in His name, could come from someone else, but He delights when we do them, because, by our doing them in His name, our faith is built up. And we are then drawn into a deeper relationship with the Father.

Let us not forget that Jesus did good works, even when it was considered unlawful to do so!

Another time Jesus went into the synagogue,

and a man with a shrivelled hand was there. Some of them were looking for a reason to accuse Jesus, so they watched him closely to see if he would heal him on the Sabbath. Jesus said to the man with the shrivelled hand, "Stand up in front of everyone." Then Jesus asked them, "Which is lawful on the Sabbath: to do good or to do evil, to save life or to kill?" But they remained silent. He looked around at them in anger and, deeply distressed at their stubborn hearts, said to the man, "Stretch out your hand." He stretched it out, and his hand was completely restored. Then the Pharisees went out and began to plot with the Herodians how they might kill Jesus. (Mark 3:1-6 NIV)

The Pharisees didn't know what to do with a law-breaker like Jesus when He performed good works.

When we do good works, this is what it means to be the hands and feet of Jesus. Feeding the poor. Handing out a water bottle to someone in the park on a hot day. Building a wheelchair ramp. Cleaning up a widow's yard overgrown with weeds and shrubs. Simply loving our neighbor.

But, please be careful. Many well intentioned folks will tell you that your good works will earn you a special place in heaven. Only God's grace and unconditional love grants us access to the eternal Kingdom.

And do you know that the word "workmanship" means that we are God's masterpieces? He is Creator. We are the created ones. Lovely. Gorgeous. Beautiful. Works of art. The best way we showcase God the creator, God the artist, is to do the good works that He has for us to do. So, let's do them out of love for the Creator! Out of love for the ability, the gift, of doing them so that His Kingdom is increased.

So, roll up those sleeves and get going. You have work to do! Receive this gift joyfully, the Gift of Work to Do on God's Behalf.

Father God, help me to be your hands and your feet today. Help me love my neighbors as I love myself. Help me to do good works in your name. Not because it will benefit me, but so that You may be glorified and so that Your Kingdom will come on this earth. In Jesus' Name. Amen.

Use this space to write a prayer or your thoughts about this Gift:

_____

_____

_____

_____

_____

_____

ADVENT DAY

6

THE GIFT OF BEING
A CITIZEN OF HEAVEN

What is the next gift God has for us? Citizenship in Heaven! Are you someone who has moved around a bunch in your life? I am. I have lived at 23 different addresses. And I didn't grow up in a military family. My average is just under two-and-a-half years per address.

So, let me tell you, I am so thankful for the gift of being a Citizen of Heaven. **"This kingdom of faith is now your home country. You're no longer strangers or outsiders. You belong here, with as much right to the name Christian as anyone."** (Ephesians 2:19 THE MESSAGE)

A few summers ago the New York Times ran a list of word phrases that are considered "The Happiest Words in the English Language." They include:

"You've been upgraded to First Class!"

"Have you lost weight?"

"It's benign."

"Let me help you."

"I love you."

When a police officer says: "Be a little more careful next time. Have a nice day."

And then there is this one ...

"In the Spring of 1971, the announcement from the cockpit of a United Airlines plane, as it was rolling into position for takeoff from Vietnam to San Francisco. There were about 250 military personnel on-board. 'The tower has already cleared us for takeoff. Let's go home.'"

"Welcome Home."[3]

Jesus has these comforting words for us: **"There are many rooms in my Father's house; I would not tell you this if it were not true. I am going there to prepare a place for you. After I go and prepare a place for you, I will come back and take you to be with me so that you may be where I am."** (John 14:1-2 NCV)

The context is similar to that of a groom in the ancient days who proposes to his bride-to-be, then returns to his family's home. He builds an addition on to that house -- a room for himself and his new bride. And when construction of the room is completed, he returns to get his bride, and they are married and return to the home he built for their new family.

It is the same for us. Isn't it great to know that no matter our wanderings, no matter our failures or successes on earth, we will always be welcomed by Jesus in heaven? That is such a great gift!

So open your arms and receive this homecoming gift this Advent, the Gift of Citizenship in Heaven.

Father, thank you for the precious gift of knowing that you have prepared a place for me to call home, in Heaven. In Jesus' name, Amen.

Use this space to write a prayer or your thoughts about this Gift:

_____

_____

_____

_____

_____

_____

_____

_____

_____

_____

_____

_____

_____

_____

_____

_____

ADVENT DAY

7

THE GIFT OF MINISTRY

One of the things that is fascinating about being a believer is that God calls each of us to act. And He does so through our spiritual wiring. Once we bow the knee to Jesus there is something that prods us along to engage others in care, compassion and service. The next Advent gift is the gift of ministry.

The Apostle Paul says it this way:

> **This is my life work: helping people understand and respond to this Message. It came as a sheer gift to me, a real surprise, God handling all the details. When it came to presenting the Message to people who had no background in God's way, I was the least qualified of any of the available Christians. God saw to it that I was equipped, but you can be sure that it had nothing to do with my natural abilities.** (Ephesians 3:7-8, THE MESSAGE)

Do you know that every believer is a minister? On the letterhead at the first church where I served, it listed all of the staff pastors. But at the top of the list it said "Ministers, Every Member." If you were an active part of the congregation you were expected to also be a minister. Not in a vocational position, but in the day to day community life of the fellowship.

That's truly how it is. Paul says if you are Gentile, or

non-Gentile, Christian or Jew, if you partake of the promises in Christ Jesus, if you have received His grace, you are a minister ... one who God will use for His Kingdom purposes.

Can people come to know Jesus in a tattoo parlor? Absolutely! There is a ministry in St. Louis that focuses just on that group of people. How about motorcycle gangs? I passed a guy on a Harley recently that had a "Bikers for Christ" patch on the back of his leather jacket. There is a Christian legal group for attorneys. There is the Christian Medical and Dental Association. There are ministries in professional sports, among airline pilots and even parents of toddlers. The list is almost endless. You name it, whatever the group of people, there are believers who are ministering to one another. And most are doing so without an ordained, pulpit pounding, seminary trained "professional minister" at the head of the organization. And that's the way God wants it.

It's a gift to be able to minister to one another with His grace. Every believer has been given the ability -- by the power of the Holy Spirit -- to listen, to pray, to encourage, to minister.

God has uniquely equipped you to minister to your neighbor. Scripture says that one of primary reasons we go through trials and difficulties is so that we can encourage others when we get to the other side of that challenge. **"Praise be to the God and Father of our Lord Jesus Christ, the Father of compassion and the God of all comfort, who comforts us in all our troubles, so that we can comfort those in any**

trouble with the comfort we ourselves receive from God.” (2 Corinthians 1:3-4 NIV)

May God continue to give you grace and blessing as you minister to one another. So, receive this gift and use it often -- the Gift of ministering to one another.

Father God, thank you for the Gift of Ministry. May the Holy Spirit lead me to minister to those who need to see your love, grace and compassion. In Jesus' Name, Amen.

Use this space to write a prayer or your thoughts about this Gift:

_____

_____

_____

_____

_____

_____

_____

_____

_____

_____

ADVENT DAY

8

THE GIFT OF BOLDNESS AND CONFIDENT ACCESS

Think back to elementary school. Did you ever get called up to the teacher's desk for a one-on-one meeting? Not a disciplinary confrontation, mind you, just a "please come here I want to talk with you" meeting. Generally, there were two opposite responses from the room full of pupils. One student would sheepishly approach the front of the classroom, head hanging low, feet shuffling along, fearful. Another student would stride confidently, chin up, eyes fixed on the teacher's eyes. The first lacked confidence, the second acted boldly.

Our next Advent gift is the Gift of Boldness!

"In him and through faith in him we may approach God with freedom and confidence." (Ephesians 3:12 NIV) The word "confidence" can be translated "boldness" or even "cheerful courage."

A friend once asked the question, "What was the difference between the disciple Peter at Passover and Peter at Pentecost?" It was 50 days and there was a 180 degree change in Peter. Recall at Passover, Peter was afraid. He acted cowardly, even lying to a young girl about his connection with Jesus. At Pentecost, in Acts 2, Peter boldly proclaimed the Gospel on the steps of the Temple for all in Jerusalem to hear. And over 3,000 responded to his sermon and were baptized that day! What was the difference? He was filled with the Holy Spirit!

Jesus, through His Holy Spirit, gives us boldness to proclaim the Gospel and also to approach the Father in Heaven to ask Him for whatever we need.

Why can we do that? In the days of Moses, man needed a mediator to go between him and Holy God. No longer, thanks to the grace of Jesus! You may recall that the moment Jesus died, the Holy of Holies in the Temple became accessible to everyone. **"At that moment the curtain of the temple was torn in two from top to bottom."** (Matthew 27:51 NIV) We now have access to the throne of God, and today's scripture says we can have **"confident access."** (Ephesians 3:12 NASB)

So ask our Father God. Receive. And boldly proclaim, with confidence. And we can have such confidence, because, as the writer of Hebrews notes **"... he who promised is faithful."** (Hebrews 10:23 NIV)

Be encouraged to use this great gift this Advent -- the gift of being able to go directly to the LORD of lords, the King of kings. The Gift of Boldness and Confident Access.

Father God, I am grateful for this gift of being able to pray directly to you. Thank you, Jesus, for tearing the veil away from the Holy of Holies. Holy Spirit, give me the boldness to proclaim the love of the Gospel. For your glory. In Jesus' name, Amen.

Use this space to write a prayer or your thoughts about this Gift:

_____

_____

_____

_____

_____

_____

_____

_____

_____

_____

_____

_____

_____

_____

_____

_____

_____

_____

9

THE GIFT OF JESUS DWELLING IN OUR HEARTS

We all know the difference between a house and a home. A house is merely a place to live. It becomes a home when those who live in the house add love. It doesn't have anything to do with the things we hang on the wall, the furniture in the family room or soft lighting in the living room. The proverb says "Home is where the heart is."

Today we receive a two-fold gift: **"I ask the Father in his great glory to give you the power to be strong inwardly through his Spirit. I pray that Christ will live in your hearts by faith and that your life will be strong in love and be built on love."** (Ephesians 3:16-17 NCV)

Paul prays for the Church here, that Believers may be strengthened by the Holy Spirit so that Christ may dwell in their hearts. The Greek word he uses for "dwell" means to "always be present." Is there a greater gift to receive than this? Christ Jesus. Living in our heart and in our life. Built on the foundation of love and strengthened by the Holy Spirit. Always present.

God can and does give us many, many things … every spiritual blessing. (Remember the first gift in this Advent study?) John Eadie, a Scottish theologian from the mid-1800's, suggests that God is not being frugal here. "His bounty proclaims His conscious possession of immeasurable resources. He bestows according to the riches of His glory -- His own infinite fullness."[4]

God gives us His all which is strengthened by the Holy Spirit so that Christ may dwell in our hearts. God no longer dwells in a building that man has made such as the tabernacle that Moses set up in the desert and moved from place to place. No. **"I heard a loud voice from the throne, saying, 'Behold, the tabernacle of God is among men, and He will dwell among them, and they shall be His people, and God Himself will be among them.'"** (Revelation 21:3 NASB) Jesus is the new tabernacle! And He dwells within us!

Jesus stresses the benefit of abiding with Him. **"I am the vine; you are the branches. If you remain in me and I in you, you will bear much fruit; apart from me you can do nothing."** (John 15:5 NIV)

Now does Jesus physically get small and live inside the muscle and tissue that is our beating heart? No. But a life that has Jesus centered in the core of our being that beats and pulses continuously with His love and grace, is a life of order and priority and purpose. As God's children, we are given everything. And that is represented in today's Gift -- Jesus Dwelling in our Spiritual Heart.

Father God, thank you that you no longer live or dwell in man-made buildings or temples, but that Jesus lives in my heart. Make my heart a loving place where He can live. In Jesus' name, Amen.

Use this space to write a prayer or your thoughts about this Gift:

_____

_____

_____

_____

_____

_____

_____

_____

_____

_____

_____

_____

_____

_____

_____

_____

_____

_____

THE GREATEST GIFTS

ADVENT DAY

10

THE GIFT OF KNOWING
HOW MUCH CHRIST LOVES US

Parents and their younger children often play the "How Much Love?" game. You know how it goes. It usually starts with Mom or Dad looking at their child and saying, "I love you." And the child looks up with big inquiring eyes, "How much do you love me?" The game continues with the parent comparing the amount of their love with the number of stars in the sky or grains of sand on the beach or the favorite in our home "to the moon and back." In the Disney movie, *Tangled*, Rapunzel's step-mother says, "I love you very much dear." To which Rapunzel replies: "I love you more." And to finish the game, her mother says "I love you most."[5]

In Ephesians 3, Paul suggests a box of love with unlimited proportions.

I pray that you and all God's holy people will have the power to understand the greatness of Christ's love -- how wide and how long and how high and how deep that love is. Christ's love is greater than anyone can ever know, but I pray that you will be able to know that love. Then you can be filled with the fullness of God. (Ephesians 3:18-19 NCV)

It is an amount of love that you just cannot get your hands around. It is reminiscent of Romans 8:35 where

Paul asks **"Who can separate us from the love of Christ?"** And then he gives us the answer a few verses later in a long list that includes **"nor height, nor depth, nor any other created thing will be able to separate us from the love of God which is in Christ Jesus our Lord."** (Romans 8:39 NASB)

How much does Christ love us? He loves us more. He loves us most. He loves us bigger than the biggest box.

If Disney's Buzz Lightyear was to answer the question, he would say "to infinity and beyond ..."[6] And that still would not be a box that could contain God's love.

And that's an awesome, incredible gift!

So, open your arms wide -- as wide as Jesus opened His for you on the cross -- and receive today's gift, the Gift of knowing how much Christ loves you!

Father God, thank you for loving me with an immeasurable amount of love. May I remember today, and every day, especially when I'm not feeling loved, that you love me more than I can comprehend. Help me receive your great love today! In Jesus' name, Amen.

Use this space to write a prayer or your thoughts about this Gift:

_____

_____

_____

_____

_____

_____

_____

_____

_____

_____

_____

_____

_____

_____

_____

_____

_____

_____

_____

ADVENT DAY

11

THE GIFT OF UNITY

Do you remember the TV show *The Waltons?* While there is no such thing as a perfect family, if there was ever an award for the perfect television family, John Boy and his ma and pa, Olivia and John, his grandparents and six brothers and sisters might have been the winners. The show was on during the 1970s. Set during the depression in rural Virginia, the Walton's lived life peaceably and with great resolve. They got along well and held up virtue to its highest esteem. Remember the love that flowed as they ended each episode? "Goodnight Grandpa. Goodnight Mary Ellen. Goodnight Jim Bob. Goodnight Pa. Goodnight Elizabeth. Goodnight John Boy."[7]

This is perhaps a picture you might see as Paul encourages the family of Christ at the beginning of Ephesians, Chapter 4.

I urge you to live a life worthy of the calling you have received. Be completely humble and gentle; be patient, bearing with one another in love. Make every effort to keep the unity of the Spirit through the bond of peace. There is one body and one Spirit, just as you were called to one hope when you were called; one Lord, one faith, one baptism; one God and Father of all, who is over all and through all and in all. (Ephesians 4:1-6 NIV)

This passage summarizes the unity that God so longs for us all to share together as the body of Christ, no matter where we go to church.

A pastor friend of mine used to say that there are some things that are disputable within the body of Christ, such as music, dress, how we raise our kids, movies, politics, that kind of thing. But there are certain things that are bedrock truths. And this is what Paul is saying here. This is the gift of unity. One body. One Spirit. One Hope. One Faith. One Baptism. One God, the Father. And right in the middle? One Lord. One. And His name is Jesus Christ! So Paul is essentially saying, "C'mon church. We can agree on this! Let's lift up the name of Christ together ... for His glory."

Have you ever travelled someplace far away, whether on a mission trip or just someplace away from home, and met another Christ-follower for the first time? There is a sweet common bond, isn't there? A unity that is shared together. And it's deeper than what your alma mater is or the sports team you root for.

You have undoubtedly heard the joke that asks the question, "What car did the disciples drive?" Acts 2:1 says that on the day of Pentecost the disciples were "all in one Accord." God bless Honda! It's an interesting picture to think of the whole church being crammed in one place, all going the same direction. In some ways, however, that *is* the picture of unity in the body of Christ.

Paul says **"Therefore if you have any encouragement from being united with Christ, if** any comfort from his love, if any common sharing in the Spirit, if any tenderness and compassion, then make my joy complete by being like-minded, having the same love, being one in spirit and of one mind." (Philippians 2:1-2 NIV)

May we be encouraged to embrace unity. No matter our race. No matter our geography. No matter our education. And may we do so in a way worthy of Christ. Being humble, gentle, patient and bearing with one another in love. May you receive, and give, this Gift of Unity this Advent.

Father God, I pray for all believers around the world today. May we all be united in bringing the Gospel message to the lost and hurting, especially during this season. May Your peace come on earth, as it is in Heaven. In Jesus' name, Amen.

Use this space to write a prayer or your thoughts about this Gift:

_____

_____

_____

_____

_____

_____

ADVENT DAY

12

THE GIFT OF GRACE

What is grace besides the prayer often offered before a meal?

Grace is a gift. And it often looks different depending upon who is giving the gift.

Have you heard the story of a man who fell down some icy steps? While he may not have been too graceful as he slipped and tumbled, he says the gift of grace looked completely different in each person that came to his rescue. The first person helped him up, examined where it hurt, took him inside and put an ice bag on the injury. This person had the grace gift of mercy. A second person came up and asked him why he hadn't properly poured salt on the icy steps before hand. This person had the grace gift of exhortation. And still a third person showed the man how to properly hold on to the hand rail and slowly work his way up each step, little by little. This person had the grace gift of teaching. Three different people, three different expressions of the same grace gift.[8]

"But to each one of us grace has been given as Christ apportioned it." (Ephesians 4:7 NIV)

"But that doesn't mean you should all look and speak and act the same. Out of the generosity of Christ, each of us is given his own gift." (Ephesians 4:7 THE MESSAGE)

Grace. Being given a second chance. And a third chance. And a fourth chance. And, as many "do-overs" as we need in order to fully accept all the love that God has for each one of us.

Some have suggested that no single man sums up the definition of grace like the man behind the song *Amazing Grace*. Do you know John Newton's story? He was a slave trader, the captain of a ship in the mid-1700s that regularly travelled the Triangle Trade Route. Beginning with an empty cargo hold in England, he would travel to Africa and pack over 600 units of "human cargo" -- slaves -- onto the ship. He would then sail to America and deliver his cargo in exchange for money and goods made in America that were needed in England. From his home in England he would rest for a short season and start all over again. He met Christ during a terrible tempest aboard his vessel. He ultimately left the seaman's life and studied for the ministry.

Near the end of his life he was pastor at the Saint Peter and Paul Church of England in Olney Parish. At age 82, Newton said, "My memory is nearly gone, but I remember two things: that I am a great sinner, and that Christ is a great Savior." He is buried in the cemetery there. On his tombstone we read these words: *John Newton, Clerk, once an infidel and libertine, a servant of slaves in Africa, was, by the rich mercy of our Lord and Saviour Jesus Christ, preserved, restored, pardoned, and appointed to preach the faith he had long labored to destroy.*[9]

Amazing Grace! What a Gift! May you be a recipient *and* a giver of this gift today.

Father God, thank you for the Gift of Grace. Thank you for the chance to start over again no matter how often. Thank you that I can receive your love new and fresh day after day after day. As you have given me grace, help me to be quick to offer it to others. In Jesus' name, Amen.

Use this space to write a prayer or your thoughts about this Gift:

_____

_____

_____

_____

_____

_____

_____

_____

_____

_____

_____

_____

_____

ADVENT DAY

13

THE GIFT OF LEARNING
WITH A PURPOSE

Have you ever visited one of the great redwood forests in California? These natural skyscrapers set records for height and girth. And they never stop growing until it's time for them to die.

How about you? Are you still growing spiritually? Or have you peaked and are just waiting until it's time to move from this life to the next? I believe that for a Christ-follower, retirement is not an option.

You've heard it said that God has a wonderful plan for your life. The idea is that we grow to fullness, maturity in the faith. Not just grow old, but grow in maturity of the faith. God does not want you to reach a certain level that you might determine on your own as "being mature" and then let you stop or coast the rest of your life. God expects growth from you, year after year, season after season, just like the giant and grand redwood trees.

I want to gently challenge and encourage you: Do you have the same level of faith you had a few years ago? Do you remember the manna that rained down on the people of Israel as they wandered through the desert for 40 years? God gave them just what they needed for that day by way of a bread-like food, each and every morning. Are you experiencing a fresh and daily delivery of manna from heaven?

Dear child, look to God to provide you with every spiritual blessing every day. Remember, that was our first gift in Ephesians 1:3. If you were to measure the relationship you have with God, is it new and fresh and growing? Or, do you take that relationship for granted? May I encourage you to press in to all that God wants you to receive each day? Even today.

God has given the body of Christ great leaders and teachers, both inside your local congregation and outside of it, or those who have gone before us whose writings can inspire and teach. He has put people on the mission field, who by their example of living for God daily in a small village, can teach us how to depend on God or how to see the miraculous move of the Holy Spirit in a way we've not seen before. All of these people have great things to teach, if you are willing to be taught.

Today's gift:

> **So Christ himself gave the apostles, the prophets, the evangelists, the pastors and teachers, to equip his people for works of service, so that the body of Christ may be built up until we all reach unity in the faith and in the knowledge of the Son of God and become mature, attaining to the whole measure of the fullness of Christ.** (Ephesians 4:11-13 NIV)

While there are a number of ways to look at this passage, I'd like to focus on the "so that" portion. God desires we become mature, attaining to the whole measure of the fullness of Christ. May I suggest that another way of saying that is "learning with a purpose."

Do you have a bucket list that includes learning new things? I hope so. May I encourage you to search out and find new ways to learn new things about how God's greatness? May I encourage you to grow in spiritual maturity? Paul says that those who are mature are not tossed here and there by the waves when trials or challenging times come. They press into the love of Christ, as the head of the body, which holds us, collectively, all together. And they do so by their willingness to be taught and encouraged by those who hold the spiritual leadership posts of Apostle, Prophet, Evangelist, Pastor, Teacher.

Every single one of us can find someone more spiritually mature than we are. Search them out and learn from them. It will strengthen you so that down the road, you might embrace the position of leadership yourself. And don't ever give up learning more and more about God's love and plan for you.

Open your hands today and receive the Gift of Learning with a Purpose. And don't ever stop. Keep growing.

Father God, help me never tire of desiring to learn more and more about you and your love and perfect plan for my life. In Jesus' name, Amen.

Use this space to write a prayer or your thoughts about this Gift:

ADVENT DAY

14

THE GIFT OF A NEW SELF, IN THE LIKENESS OF GOD

Today's gift from God is a three-part gift. **"... and to put on the new self, created to be like God in true righteousness and holiness."** (Ephesians 4:24 NIV)

Putting on the new self. It can't really happen until you, Part 1, take off the old self and then, Part 2, renew your mind, for Part 3, putting on the new self.

Are you a collector? Do you have things around the house that really have no value at all? I confess, I'm one of those people. I used to collect all sorts of things. Baseball cards. Vintage 45 records. Pop bottles. License plates. The front pages from old newspapers with memorable headlines. I'm sure when I decided to keep these things there was a reason. But today I have to wonder why I keep them. They just take up valuable storage space.

We all have some old junk in our lives. Throughout this chapter Paul takes the reader through a long list of old junk we need get rid of if we are to live the full life that God has for us: impure sensuality, greed, stealing, unwholesome talk, bitterness, wrath, anger, slander. Get rid of it. Renew your mind.

That is a tremendous gift! Once we say "yes" to being a Christ-follower, we get to get rid of the junk and live a life in the likeness of God! In your old self you might have had the label "adulterer," "thief," "loser," or "addict." But guess what? That's not you anymore! What a beautiful gift! It's like putting on a gorgeous new dress or an Armani suit.

I visited my mom a few years ago while I was on a business trip. I was on my way to a meeting all dressed up in an Italian suit and ready to tackle the business of the day. But I first took a detour to drive with my mom to one of her weekly Bible studies. One dear woman, when seeing me for the first time in probably 20 years, exclaimed: "You look like a million bucks!" Isn't it great to look like a million bucks? But let me tell you, when you are a new creation in Christ, your value to our Lord is always "priceless."

I think that one of reasons we collect stuff is because we hope that someday it will be worth something. We can sell it on craigslist or on eBay. And we think, if this thing is worth something and I own this thing, then I am worth something.

May I tell you something? Once you put off the old and put on the new self, in the likeness of Christ, you are the wealthiest you will ever be! Your Father owns the cattle on a thousand hills. You have been given every spiritual blessing. You can't get any wealthier!

Here's how The Message summarizes this gift:

Everything -- and I do mean everything -- connected with that old way of life has to go. It's rotten through and through. Get rid of it! And then take on an entirely new way of life -- a God-fashioned life, a life renewed from the

inside and working itself into your conduct as God accurately reproduces his character in you. (Ephesians 4:24, THE MESSAGE)

God wants to reproduce His character in you! And it's beautiful when you let Him do it! It's a beautiful, priceless gift!

Get dressed up for today's gift -- the Gift of a New Self, in the Likeness of God.

Father God, thank you that I am priceless in your sight. Thank you for the Gift of a New Self, created in your image. Help me receive this gift every single day, even today! In Jesus' name, Amen.

Use this space to write a prayer or your thoughts about this Gift:

_____

_____

_____

_____

_____

_____

_____

_____

ADVENT DAY

15

THE GIFT OF CHRIST HIMSELF, AN OFFERING, A SACRIFICE

Do you know that smell is one of the senses that can trigger a very specific memory? It's weird, but I still remember the smell of our new, plastic telephones in our brand new home in 1967. Can you remember your grandmother's perfume? Or how about the leather smell of the saddle of your first horse or new car? A certain flower? A visit to a different country? I can tell you from personal experience that Bombay, India in late June has a different smell than the mountains of Switzerland in the spring time.

What is the most pleasant fragrance you've ever smelled?

One year at Bibletimes Marketplace, our children's summer Bible school event, one of the workshop leaders talked about the fragrance of the burnt offerings by the Old Testament priests. To recreate the event he took some seasonings, popular in the Middle East, like cumin and paprika, and mixed in some rosemary plants and rose petals, and threw it in a fire. What a beautiful and amazing aroma it was! And can you imagine the additional flavor similar to smoked brisket as the carcasses of bulls or rams were offered to the Lord? The Bible suggests that such fragrant offerings were pleasing to God.

Today's gift if the gift of Christ Himself.

"Walk in the way of love, just as Christ loved us and gave himself up for us as a fragrant offering and sacrifice to God." (Ephesians 5:2 NIV)

Paul writes that Christ loved us so much, He gave himself up for us, an offering and a sacrifice to God as a fragrant aroma.

It's hard for most of us to get our heads around the sacrifice of Jesus, God's Son, and that such an offering was pleasing to God. Pause and think about that for a second.

There are two things to ponder here as it relates to the sacrifice of Jesus. The first is that a true sacrifice is one that is offered by oneself. In the Old Testament, Leviticus Chapter 1 has certain rules about offering a sacrifice. The first is this: when a man offered bulls or birds, Leviticus says he did the actual killing himself. And then, he gave the slain animal to the priest. There is a reason for that. You must offer your own sacrifice to identify with the killing of life.

The second rule from Leviticus as it relates to sacrifice is that the one making the offering is to skin the animal and give the meat to the priest to burn. But the skin is offered to the priest to keep as a robe. This is so significant! God had to kill and skin an animal to cover Adam and Eve's nakedness in Genesis, Chapter 3, to cover their sinfulness. In the same way, the offering, the sacrifice of Christ, clothes us in righteousness. God doesn't see our sin when He looks at us, He sees the righteousness of Jesus, clothing us in a garment of praise, with a beautiful aroma that is pleasing to the

Lord our God.

So this Gift of Christ Himself -- an offering, a sacrifice -- is, indeed, the greatest of all gifts.

Receive this gift today -- the Gift of our Lord Jesus!

Father God, I give my heart to Jesus today! Thank you for this most wonderful Gift. Thank you for the sacrifice He gave to clothe me in His righteousness. May my life give off the sweet aroma of the love of Jesus to everyone I meet today. In Jesus' name, Amen.

Use this space to write a prayer or your thoughts about this Gift:

_____

_____

_____

_____

_____

_____

_____

_____

ADVENT DAY

16

THE GIFT OF ENCOURAGEMENT

When you feel a need for encouragement, what do you do? Do you call someone special? Do you exercise or paint or play a game with your son or daughter? How about singing or dancing or just watching a play or a movie? Or maybe it's just connecting with a good friend over coffee or tossing a ball to your dog.

We all need encouragement from time to time, don't we?

Today's gift is what I see to be the Gift of Encouragement. It's probably just the way I'm wired, but I see encouragement all through the paragraph that begins with Verse 18 of Chapter 5:

Do not get drunk on wine, which leads to debauchery. Instead, be filled with the Spirit, speaking to one another with psalms, hymns, and songs from the Spirit. Sing and make music from your heart to the Lord, always giving thanks to God the Father for everything, in the name of our Lord Jesus Christ. (Ephesians 5:18-20 NIV)

Within the past year or so I took a spiritual connection assessment. It asked a series of questions about how one connects with God. Some people connect with God best by being out in nature; some in quiet solitude. For me, my strongest connection with God is in worship. I love to worship and sing my heart out and I love those musicians who lead worship and so skillfully take us to a place of complete adoration of God. And truly, when one is fully immersed in worship, I can understand how Paul connects it with being drunk. And I see this as a gift of encouragement in that he says "to speak to one another with psalms ..."

The Psalms are a fabulous source of Spirit-filled encouragement. Many are David's personal journal entries. I can so relate to David. Often he begins a Psalm with a cry: **"Save me, O God, for the waters have threatened my life! I have sunk in deep mire, and there is no foothold ... I am weary with my crying ... I wait for my God ..."** (Psalm 69:1, 3 NASB) And then, as he journals and writes and ponders the greatness of God's blessings through the next several verses, more than likely in song, the Holy Spirit takes him to a place of adoration at the conclusion. **"Let heaven and earth praise Him!"** (Psalm 69:34 NASB)

May I encourage you to encourage one another, through the words of the Psalms, or through other places of Scripture? Write them out as prayers and give them to one another and encourage one another. That is the true Gift of Encouragement! God gave us His word, filled with songs of blessings. Yes, you can read them yourself. However, isn't it great when God gives you a word of Scripture that He wants you to share with someone else? Or He directs someone to a specific passage and they write it down and give it to you? This is how the body is built up.

Mary, the mother of Jesus, answered the call of her

destiny with a song and a word of encouragement. Following her encounter with the angel Gabriel, and as she met with her cousin Elizabeth -- who was also supernaturally pregnant, carrying her son, John the Baptizer -- Mary quotes the Old Testament song of Hannah from 1 Samuel 2.

"I'm bursting with God-news! I'm walking on air. I'm laughing at my rivals. I'm dancing my salvation. Nothing and no one is holy like God ..." (1 Samuel 2: 1-2 and Luke 1:46 THE MESSAGE)

The words of both Mary and Hannah! That is sheer joy and encouragement all in one!

May you receive this Gift of Spirit-filled Encouragement and be available to give this Gift to others during this Advent season.

Father God, thank you for those who encourage me when I need to be encouraged. Thank you for blessing me with every spiritual blessing. May I be both a giver and a receiver this Advent. In Jesus' name, Amen.

Use this space to write a prayer or your thoughts about this Gift:

_____

_____

_____

_____

_____

_____

_____

_____

_____

_____

_____

_____

_____

_____

_____

_____

_____

ADVENT DAY

17

THE GIFT OF FAMILY

Did you know that researchers have found that people who are married have a better life? Yes, it's true! Many may find holes in the data to support their own experience, however, if you are married there is a strong likelihood that you will live a longer life, have a better financial picture, and enjoy better mental health and greater safety than those who are not married.[10]

From my perspective, this data supports God's perfect plan all along. Today's gift from Ephesians is the Gift of Family.

Here's how The Message describes the key relationship of wives and husbands, beginning in Ephesians 5:21:

Out of respect for Christ, be courteously reverent to one another.

Wives, understand and support your husbands in ways that show your support for Christ. The husband provides leadership to his wife the way Christ does to his church, not by domineering but by cherishing. So just as the church submits to Christ as he exercises such leadership, wives should likewise submit to their husbands.

Husbands, go all out in your love for your wives, exactly as Christ did for the church -- a

love marked by giving, not getting. Christ's love makes the church whole. His words evoke her beauty. Everything he does and says is designed to bring the best out of her, dressing her in dazzling white silk, radiant with holiness. And that is how husbands ought to love their wives. They're really doing themselves a favor -- since they're already "one" in marriage.
(Ephesians 5:21-28, THE MESSAGE)

Paul's definition of marriage is the way God would like it to be for us. That's the way it *can* be. It's not just a pipe dream or an awesome goal. With the Holy Spirit in us and encouraging us daily, it *can* be that way.

A good marriage takes a lot of hard work. A good family life even more work. It is understandable to say that you may feel like you've put out all the hard work you can muster at your job and that there just isn't enough time or energy left to make your marriage work like God intended.

Someone once said that marriage is not a 50-50 proposition, in that each spouse does 50% of the work. No, marriage is a 100-100 proposition. Both the husband and the wife are to pour 100% of their energies into making it work.

One could drone on and on about what makes a good marriage and what makes a bad marriage, citing wedding vows and divorce statistics. It's not that simple. Life *is* complex. It is complicated as a single adult. It's more challenging as a couple. And it gets really interesting when that couple adds some children into that life. But what a gift your family can be! What a joy our children are! Especially when we take the time to see them as God does.

Billy Graham's parenting advice: "Children will invariably talk, eat, walk, think, respond, and act like their parents. Give them a target to shoot at. Give them a goal to work toward. Give them a pattern that they can see clearly, and you give them something that gold and silver cannot buy."[11]

Marriage, and family, is a great gift! Make a little time this season to read Ephesians 5:22 through 6:4 and ponder how you can be a better parent, or a better son or daughter, in your family. Ask God to give you His grace and His eyes to see your family members the way He does. That is a wonderful gift!

Father God, thank you for the Gift of my family. Help me see the members of my family the way you do. Use me to bring your peace and your grace and your love to my family this Season. In Jesus' name, Amen.

Use this space to write a prayer or your thoughts about this Gift:

_____

_____

_____

ADVENT DAY

18

THE GIFT OF VICTORY
OVER THE ENEMY

Desert Storm. The Iraqi Desert, just north of Kuwait. 1991. You may remember this first of the most recent wars being fought with American troops in the oil-field rich Middle East. Saddam Hussein had pushed into neighboring Kuwait. And the United States and its Ally nations were not going to let Iraq set a precedent of bullying smaller nations. As the US Forces surged north across the desert sands, one defensive strategy used by the evil dictator was to set on fire all of the oil pumping units. A large, oil rich, toxic smoke began to form. Our US troops were puzzled and worried. Gas masks were issued to all soldiers; most of the armed men or women wondered if the protective devices would work. The weather forecasters studied the skies as the black cloud moved its way toward the ground troops.

Heavy casualties were predicted. However, 15 minutes before the beginning of the largest ground assault of the attack, just before 4 a.m. on February 24, 1991, the winds changed and began to push that toxic, black, oil-rich smoke north, instead of south. Many troops say that God had performed a miracle on their behalf.[12] One of countless miracles He performed during that war. And as anyone who has been on the front lines of any battle can tell you, God regularly shows up in battle situations.

He shows up in our daily battles, too. When we ask for

His divine intervention and when we take the initiative to gear up and fight, His presence is assured!

Today's Christmas gift from God is the Gift of Victory over the Enemy.

"Finally, be strong in the Lord and in the strength of His might." (Ephesians 6:10 NASB)

Paul is starting the conclusion of his letter to the church at Ephesus. He has encouraged them, instructed them, taught them, prayed for them. Now his last words are to charge them. "Be strong!" Reach into that inner core. Rely on the Holy Spirit to guide and strengthen you.

Because, really, this is not pretty.

He describes a battle here. A vicious, ugly, full of blood, sweat and tears battle.

> **This is no afternoon athletic contest that we'll walk away from and forget about in a couple of hours. This is for keeps, a life-or-death fight to the finish against the Devil and all his angels. Be prepared. You're up against far more than you can handle on your own. Take all the help you can get, every weapon God has issued, so that when it's all over but the shouting you'll still be on your feet.** (Ephesians 6:12-13 THE MESSAGE)

Paul says that our life is not merely a short-term event. Not a 15-round boxing bout or a 60-minute football game. Our lifelong struggle is **"against the rulers, against the powers, against the world forces**

of this darkness, against the spiritual forces of wickedness." (Ephesians 6:12 NASB) This is real. This is for keeps. Satan hates you and everything you are doing for God's glory. And he wants to take you down. He wants to take your marriage down. He wants to take your family down. And he'll use whatever is going on in your current situation to beat you up.

Perhaps, you've had a misunderstanding with your spouse, so you start daydreaming about what it'd be like to not be married. You bounced a check, so you start fearing any and every decision that has to do with money. Your mom yelled at you, and you start thinking how great it'd be if you never talked with her again. You have two choices: take the lazy way out and acquiesce and give in and say "so what?" and just ride the tide. Or, you can fight. I'd like to encourage you to fight. Fight for what is right. It's worth it. You are worth it. The people in your life are worth it.

So, receive the Gift of Victory! It's a true joy.

Father God, thank you for the Gift of being able to defeat the enemy. Give me what I need to stand fast and firm and strong. Holy Spirit, help me make right decisions that honor God so that the enemy will not be able to defeat me. In Jesus' name, Amen.

Use this space to write a prayer or your thoughts about this Gift:

_____

_____

_____

_____

_____

_____

_____

_____

_____

_____

_____

_____

_____

_____

_____

_____

_____

_____

_____

_____

ADVENT DAY

19

THE GIFT OF WEAPONRY, THE BELT OF TRUTH

There are many great kernels of wisdom parents can pass along to their children. One of my favorites and one that has become a favorite of my now adult children: "A half truth is a whole lie." It's important that children learn to tell the truth, right?

Truth is at the core of the judicial system. Think about the vow that someone takes when testifying in a court of law. They agree to "tell the truth, the whole truth and nothing but the truth."

So, how significant is it then that the first piece of weaponry, of armor, that Paul writes about in Ephesians Chapter 6 is the encouragement to put on the belt of truth? The truth is the leading weapon used to defeat the enemy!

"Stand firm then, with the belt of truth buckled around your waist." (Ephesians 6:14 NIV)

Circle yourself with truth. Don't mess with the half-truths of the world. Don't buy the lies of Hollywood and Madison Avenue. A good start to defeating the enemy is to not fool around with the father of lies!

I'm reminded of another piece of advice from Paul. **"Finally, brothers and sisters, whatever is true, whatever is noble, whatever is right, whatever is pure, whatever is lovely, whatever is admirable --**

if anything is excellent or praiseworthy -- think about such things." (Philippians 4:8 NIV)

The belt. It wraps around your center of gravity. It is the physical center of who you are. Let your life be balanced with the truth. Let it be your spiritual center, too. Surround yourself with the truth and people who are people of truth and who will be ones who speak truth into your life. Let every part of you be enveloped with truth.

The truth is "Weapon Number One" to defeat the attacks of the enemy. When you may be confused or unsure, get the facts. Get to the truth. Who is the truth? Jesus is the truth. **"Jesus answered, 'I am the way and the truth and the life. No one comes to the Father except through me.'"** (John 14:6 NIV)

The Bible is full of many truths about who you are. Open your Bible, open your eyes, open your hands and receive the Gift of Truth this Advent.

Father God, thank you for the Gift of Truth. May I circle every area of my life with it. In Jesus' name, Amen.

Use this space to write a prayer or your thoughts about this Gift:

ADVENT DAY

20

THE GIFT OF WEAPONRY, THE BREASTPLATE OF RIGHTEOUSNESS

There is a song by Francesca Battistelli called *Be Born in Me*. It has been the cry of the heart of our family the past few years at Christmas time. There is a line in the chorus that says "I'll hold you in the beginning. You will hold me in the end. Every moment in the middle, make my heart your Bethlehem."[13]

What does it mean to "make my heart your Bethlehem?" Well, if we say that Bethlehem is the place where Jesus was born, we are saying to God, "Make my heart a place where Jesus is born, where he lives."

If we dig into the story of Bethlehem, we learn that Bethlehem was also the City of David, the place where the young shepherd boy tended his flock and where he later downed a giant named Goliath with a single stone. It is where David was anointed by Samuel. It was also where Ruth gleaned wheat from nearby fields. Ruth was David's grandmother.

Bethlehem means "House of Bread." It makes sense then, that Jesus was born here for He said that He is "the true bread from heaven" and "the bread of life" (John, Chapter 6). He also fed thousands with a few loaves of bread.

Jesus came from the House of Bread to give us life, true bread, true sustenance. Jesus is all we really need. He satisfies our greatest hunger and strengthens us spiritually, just as bread does physically. What happens when you don't eat for a few days? You become weak, right? What happens when you don't feast on the Bread of Life daily? You become spiritually weak, and you give the enemy an opportunity to break into your spirit and your heart.

So how do you protect your heart? **"Stand firm then, ... with the breastplate of righteousness in place."** (Ephesians 6:14 NIV)

Where do we get our righteousness? Only by affirming the grace-saving love of Jesus. You see, by dying for us, Jesus' sacrifice is our covering of righteousness, like when the Old Testament priests offered sacrifices for sin.

In this text, Paul is actually saying that accepting Jesus into our heart is one of the weapons of spiritual warfare that will keep us spiritually strong.

It's also the reason that Satan hates you.

So, cover your heart with the righteousness of Christ. Protect your heart. Don't give the enemy your heart. Satan will use worldly "love" to get to you. He will use fleshly "love," or more appropriately lust, to get to you. It's one of his most successful schemes.

Your heart belongs to Christ. He bought it with His sacrifice.

Receive this great Gift of God's Righteousness and may it protect your heart.

Father God, my prayer is that Jesus will be born in my heart. And may His sacrifice be my righteousness. And may it cover and protect me from the enemy. In Jesus' name, Amen.

Use this space to write a prayer or your thoughts about this Gift:

_____

_____

_____

_____

_____

_____

_____

_____

_____

_____

_____

_____

_____

21

THE GIFT OF WEAPONRY, THE BOOTS OF READINESS TO SHARE THE GOSPEL

"I have good news and bad news; which do you want to hear first?" When faced with that question, which do you choose?

Today's gift is the Gift of Good News. And that gift is strong and powerful and will defeat the enemy in your life. It's a key piece of the full armor of God. **"On your feet wear the Good News of peace to help you stand strong."** (Ephesians 6:15 NCV)

Like the previous two pieces of armor, Paul is actually quoting from the Old Testament text in describing these weapons of warfare. This is a reference from a famous passage in Isaiah: **"How lovely on the mountains are the feet of him who brings good news, who announces peace and brings good news of happiness, who announces salvation, and says to Zion, 'Your God reigns!'"** (Isaiah 52:7 NASB)

Did you know that in the ancient days there were messengers who delivered news after battles of war? Some were messengers of good news. Some were messengers of bad news.[14] The commanders at the back of battle actually knew, from a distance, by who was coming, whether the news was good or bad.

Paul essentially says, "Be a messenger of good news. Bring peace. Bring happiness. Bring salvation." When you enter a room, do you bring peace and blessing? Or do you add anxiety and stress to your conversations?

I'm reminded of Peter's words, **"Always be prepared to give an answer to everyone who asks you to give the reason for the hope that you have. Do this with gentleness and respect."** (1 Peter 3:15 NIV)

Or from Paul in his letter to the Romans: **"If possible, so far as it depends on you, be at peace with all men."** (Romans 12:18 NASB)

Avoid conflict. Be at peace. Don't major in the minor stuff. Be quick to forgive. Be a messenger of peace. Will your boots get muddy sometimes? Yes, most certainly. Jesus was born in a dirty cave. He came to get messy because our lives are messy. But we can still bring peace, even with mud on our boots. Especially with mud on our boots.

Peacefulness. It's a joyous Gift to give and receive this Christmas.

Father God, help me to be one who brings peace into a room, not anxiety or bad news about others. Make me a messenger of Your perfect peace and Your good news. In Jesus' name, Amen.

Use this space to write a prayer or your thoughts about this Gift:

ADVENT DAY

22

THE GIFT OF WEAPONRY,
THE SHIELD OF FAITH

"And also use the shield of faith with which you can stop all the burning arrows of the Evil One." (Ephesians 6:16 NCV)

What an interesting picture this is! First of all, when I think of Roman soldiers and their shields, I think of them using the shield to protect against swords and maces, in hand-to-hand combat, not flaming arrows. Think about flaming arrows. They must be shot at you from quite a distance, right? You probably can see them from a long way off, right? I think that is good news, even great news! If you are child of Christ, if you have any faith in Him, you can first acknowledge that there is a battle going on. But dear child of God, please know that you are always closer to Jesus than you are to Satan. Let me say that again: you are always closer to Jesus than you are to the enemy. You will always be supernaturally protected by the closeness of God.

What is faith? **"Faith makes us sure of what we hope for and gives us proof of what we cannot see."** (Hebrews 11:1 CEV)

Hold up that faith shield. Believe in what you can't see, and in doing so, you will see God in a real way.

If you are a new creation in Christ, then you are born of God, you are His child, His heir. Look at the reference to "faith" in 1 John:

"Everyone who is a child of God conquers the world. And this is the victory that conquers the world -- our faith. So the one who conquers the world is the person who believes that Jesus is the Son of God." (1 John 5:4-5 NCV)

So, our faith, your faith, conquers the world! What a great gift!

And that fits right in with Jesus own words: "I told you these things so that you can have peace in me. In this world you will have trouble, but be brave! I have defeated the world." (John 16:33 NCV)

Receive and use this gift to help you defeat the enemy and the lies he throws at you. Deflect them with your shield of faith.

Father God, thank you for the Gift of Faith. Would you please increase my faith in you? Would you help me use this gift to defeat the enemy? And thank you that you are always closer to me than Satan. In Jesus' name, Amen.

Use this space to write a prayer or your thoughts about this Gift:

_____

_____

_____

_____

_____

_____

_____

_____

_____

_____

_____

_____

_____

_____

_____

_____

_____

_____

_____

ADVENT DAY

23

THE GIFT OF WEAPONRY, THE HELMET OF SALVATION

The next piece of armor covers your head. We've surrounded our waist with truth, covered our feet with peace, and have protected our heart with the grace of Jesus. We have lifted high the shield of faith and have been reminded that God is always closer to us than the enemy.

Next: Ephesians 6:17 -- The Helmet of Salvation. You are saved from your head to your toes. Be wise, wear a helmet! Protect your mind.

In the past 20 years or so, helmets have become a standard part our daily routine. When I learned to ride a bicycle, I never wore a helmet. And I had an accident or two and banged my head from time to time (maybe that's why I'm the way I am?). But these days, you wouldn't think of teaching your child to ride a bike without first wearing a helmet. Small babies wear helmets. Why, even cowboys and bull riders are wearing helmets instead of cowboy hats. Why? Because they work! They protect your head. They keep you safe. Have you read recently of all the research and technology put into the new NFL football helmets? There are molded shells and something called TPU padding. There is a lot of science going into protecting players' heads. They've come a long way from the leather-heads of the early days of football.

Construction workers, athletes of all types, soldiers, firefighters ... all wear helmets. Whether they look cool or not, they protect your head.

Paul says make sure you know every day that your salvation saves you, protects you, keeps you in the game and keeps you mentally alert.

And how do you get your salvation? That's the same question the Roman jailer asked Paul and Silas. Their answer? **"Believe in the Lord Jesus and you will be saved."** (Acts 16:31 NCV)

And think about Paul's words in Romans as it relates to transforming our mind, which is the key central point in all of our decision making. How do you know what God's will is? **"Do not conform any longer to the pattern of this world, but be transformed by the renewing of your mind. Then you will be able to test and approve what God's will is -- his good, pleasing and perfect will."** (Romans 12:2 NIV) How do you renew your mind? By transforming your thinking. And how do you transform your thinking? By meditating on God and His word and His promises for you.

Transform your mind. Defeat the enemy.

Keep your head and your thoughts protected. Be safe. Wear a helmet! Enjoy this Gift, His Helmet of Salvation.

Father God, thank you for the Gift of protection for my mind. Thank you for your Word which renews my thinking. May I dwell on you and your thoughts today. In Jesus' name, Amen.

Use this space to write a prayer or your thoughts about this Gift:

_____

_____

_____

_____

_____

_____

_____

_____

_____

_____

_____

_____

_____

_____

_____

ADVENT DAY

24

THE GIFT OF WEAPONRY,
THE SWORD OF THE SPIRIT

There is an interesting story of the great evangelist and reformer, Martin Luther, who founded the Lutheran and Protestant faiths. There was a stain on the floor in his study at Wartburg Castle. When giving tours, the guide would remark that the stain occurred when Luther threw his ink bottle at the devil. In his later years, Luther was hounded by the enemy, and had seasons of depression and mood swings, which he called evil spirits.

In *The Seal and Pledge of the Holy Spirit*, Brian Allison reports:

> The devil sought to discourage [Luther], by making him feel guilty, through rehearsing a list of his sins. When the devil had finished, Luther purportedly said, "Think harder: you must have forgotten some." And the devil did think, and he listed more sins. When he was done enumerating the sins, Luther said, "Now, with a red pen write over that list, "The blood of Jesus Christ, God's Son, cleanses us from all sin." The devil had nothing to say.[15]

Luther threw ink at the enemy. It was his way of tangibly saying, "The Word of God is stronger!"

It is perhaps easy to suggest that in Luther's own defense against the enemy he was strongly influenced by Jesus himself. In both Matthew 4 and Luke 4 when

Jesus was tempted by the enemy, Jesus was victorious because He threw words of scripture, the words of truth, back at the devil.

Today's gift is the only offensive weapon in the full armor. Please see the significance in that. **"… and the sword of the Spirit, which is the word of God."** (Ephesians 6:17 NIV)

Look at how Jesus used this weapon. He is tired. He is hungry. He has been fasting for 40 days.

> **The devil came to Jesus to tempt him, saying, "If you are the Son of God, tell these rocks to become bread." Jesus answered: "It is written in the Scriptures, 'A person lives not on bread alone, but by everything God says.'"** (Matthew 4:3-4 NCV)

Jesus is actually quoting Moses here:

> **Remember how the Lord your God has led you in the desert for these forty years, taking away your pride and testing you, because he wanted to know what was in your heart. He wanted to know if you would obey his commands. He took away your pride when he let you get hungry, and then he fed you with manna, which neither you nor your ancestors had ever seen. This was to teach you that a person does not live on bread alone, but by everything the Lord says.** (Deuteronomy 8:2-3 NCV)

Two additional times when the enemy tempts Jesus, the

Master uses the Word of God as an offensive weapon to defeat the devil.

So, if the sword of the spirit, which is the Word of God, worked for Jesus, it will certainly work for you.

But, did Jesus have his Torah handy or his internet bookmarked at *biblegateway.com*? No, it was written on His heart. He had memorized scripture. This should give us all great motivation to learn scripture so that we can be appropriately on the offense when attacked by the enemy.

Do you know that most Jewish boys and girls, even today, have memorized the Torah -- the first five books of the Bible: Genesis, Exodus, Leviticus, Numbers and Deuteronomy -- by the time they are 12 years old! Twelve!

Maybe scripture memory would be a great new goal for next year? You don't have to memorize the Torah, but some key scriptures would be ideal. There are many, but *Bible.org* has a great resource to help you.[16] The Navigators organization has a Topical Memory System that is also good.[17] And a great Christian art company called OpticalJoy has "Sword of the Spirit" cards to encourage you and others in memorizing and sharing God's word.[18]

So pick up your sword, your Bible. Be ready to use this gift and be on the offensive. In that way you'll defeat the father of lies and encourage others with the love of God that is at its core.

Father God, thank you for this Gift, the Word of God. May I write your Word on my heart. Help me to use this gift to defeat the enemy and to build up and encourage my friends and family. May I find the Bible to be a delightful source of personal strength, love and grace. In Jesus' name, Amen.

Use this space to write a prayer or your thoughts about this Gift:

_____

_____

_____

_____

_____

_____

_____

_____

_____

_____

_____

_____

ADVENT DAY

25

THE GIFT OF PRAYER

Paul's final gift for us this Advent is the Gift of Prayer. Ephesians 6:18 says, **"pray at all times in the Spirit"** and Verse 19 **"pray for me."**

Pray at all times. Sounds remarkably like 1Thessalonians 5:17 **"Pray without ceasing"** Doesn't it?

Pray in the Spirit. That sounds a lot like Romans 8:26, which says that when we don't know how to pray or what to pray, **"… the Spirit helps us with our weakness. We do not know how to pray as we should. But the Spirit himself speaks to God for us, even begs God for us with deep feelings that words cannot explain."** (Romans 8:26 NCV)

Is there any greater gift to open on this Christmas Day, other than the gift of the Christ-child Himself, than the ability to be able to connect with our Holy Father, God, in prayer?

And what a sweet gift it is to be able to offer prayers on behalf of others.

There are countless stories of answered prayer. One of my favorites is from George Muller who served the Lord over 150 years ago. He was a man who took seriously the charge of God to take care of widows and orphans. Throughout his life, he reportedly cared for over 10,000 orphans. He was characterized as a man of prayer. It is said he prayed about everything and expected each prayer to be answered. He never asked anyone, other than God, for funds to operate over 100 different homes for children in England and throughout Europe.

From his journal:

During the summer and autumn of 1866 we had also the measles at all the three Orphan-Houses. After they had made their appearance, our especial prayer was:

1. That there might not be too many children ill at one time in this disease, so that our accommodation in the Infirmary rooms or otherwise might be sufficient. This prayer was answered to the full; for though we had at the New Orphan-House Number 1 not less than 83 cases, in Number 2 altogether 111, and in Number 3 altogether 68; yet God so graciously was pleased to listen to our supplications, as that when our spare rooms were filled with the invalids, He so long stayed the spreading of the measles till a sufficient number were restored, so as to make room for others, who were taken ill.

2. Further we prayed, that the children, who were taken ill in the measles, might be safely brought through and not die. Thus it was. We had the full answer to our prayers; for though 262 children altogether had the measles, not one of them died.

3. Lastly we prayed, that no evil physical consequences might follow this disease, as is so

often the case; this was also granted. All the 262 children not only recovered, but did well afterwards. I gratefully record this signal mercy and blessing of God, and this full and precious answer to prayer, to the honor of His name.[19]

Two-hundred sixty-two children with the measles in an orphanage. In the 1860s. None of them died. That's unheard of! A true answer to prayer.

It is a gift to be able to pray and it is a joy to see how God answers our prayers! And may I encourage you that when you feel like you have prayed and prayed and prayed and you have not seen God's answer, to keep praying and to keep looking for Him. He will answer you. In His time and by His will. And He will answer with what is best for you and the situation. You may not be able to see that His answer is best, but trust it. In time, you will see the mighty and loving hand of our Father God. And what a gift!

So, when you feel like a cloud is over you, like our soldiers did in Desert Storm, when you feel attacked by the enemy, gear up. Pray up. God is here for you.

And the most tangible gift of His presence is in the Gift we celebrate today, Jesus. Merry Christmas!

Father God, thank you for the Gift of Prayer ... to be able to talk with you and seek your face. Thank you. Help me trust that you are answering my prayers, in your timing and by your will. May I be able to see that you only want what is best for me. In Jesus' name, Amen.

Use this space to write a prayer or your thoughts about this **Gift**:

I trust you've enjoyed spending a few minutes each day during this gift giving and receiving season to get a closer look at the love and gifts God has for you, as revealed by Paul in his letter to the Church at Ephesus. Merry Christmas!

Always welcome and appreciate your feedback. Please feel free to email or write: **richronald@att.net**.

Rich Ronald
8718 Oak Ledge Drive
San Antonio, TX 78217

If you've enjoyed this book, please feel free to write a review on my author's page at *Amazon.com*.

END NOTES

1. Clinebell, H.J. (1992). Well Being: A Personal Plan for Exploring and Enriching the Seven Dimensions of Life: Mind, Body, Spirit, Love Work, Play, the World. New York, NY: Harper Collins.

2. John Calvin, The Third Sermon on the First Chapter of Ephesians. Calvin's Ephesians' Sermons, preached on Sundays at Geneva in 1558-59, when he was 49 years of age, were first printed in French in 1562, then in English in 1577. the-highway.com.

3. NY Times, August 30, 2010, schott.blogs.nytimes.com/2010/08/30/welcome-home/

4. preceptaustin.org/ephesians_316-17.htm

5. *Tangled*, produced by Walt Disney Animation Studios and Walt Disney Pictures, 2010.

6. *Toy Story*, produced by Pixar Animation Studios and Walt Disney Pictures, 1995.

7. *The Waltons*, produced by Lorimar Productions, 1971.

8. Ed Taylor, Spiritual Gifts, February, 2002.

9. joyfulheart.com/misc/newton.htm

10. The Case for Marriage, by Linda Waite and Maggie Gallagher, 2001, Broadway Press.

11. Billy Graham, The Hour of Decision, 1958.

12. Personal meetings and email messages from Ken Mahnke, USAF retired, a member of the Desert Storm ground troops. Also, various news stories in the press confirm these details.

13. *Be Born in Me* words and music by Bernie Herms and Nichole Nordeman, recorded by Francesca Battistelli. Copyright© 2011 Birdboy Songs (ASCAP) Bernie Herms Music (BMI) Birdwing Music (ASCAP Emi Cmg Music) (BMI) (adm. At EMICMGPublisching.com) All rights reserved.

14. godrules.net/library/clarke/clarkeisa52.htm

15. redeemer-lutheran.net/Articles/1000039345/ Redeemer_Lutheran_Church/Media_Center/ Pastors_Articles/Throwing_Ink_at.aspx

16. bible.org/article/advanced-scripture-memory-program

17. www.navpress.com/Topical-Memory-System/ dp/1576839974#sthash.SJKvapjv.dpbs

18. www.opticaljoy.com/browse_sos_cards/

19. *Answers to Prayer*, p. 63, from George Muller's Narratives, compiled by A.E.C. Brooks, Published by Moody Press, Chicago.

ABOUT THE AUTHOR

Rich Ronald loves to encourage others. He has a diverse background that includes television news, youth ministry and medical marketing. He is currently the Satellite Campus Minister for Oak Hills Church, North Central Campus in San Antonio, Texas. He attended Southern Baptist Theological Seminary. You can follow his blog at *www.richlyspeaking.com*. Rich has been married to his dear bride, Linda, for 26 years. They have two sons and a daughter. This is his second book. The first, *Be Born in Me,* is also a Christmas season devotional, published in 2012.

Made in the USA
San Bernardino, CA
13 October 2014